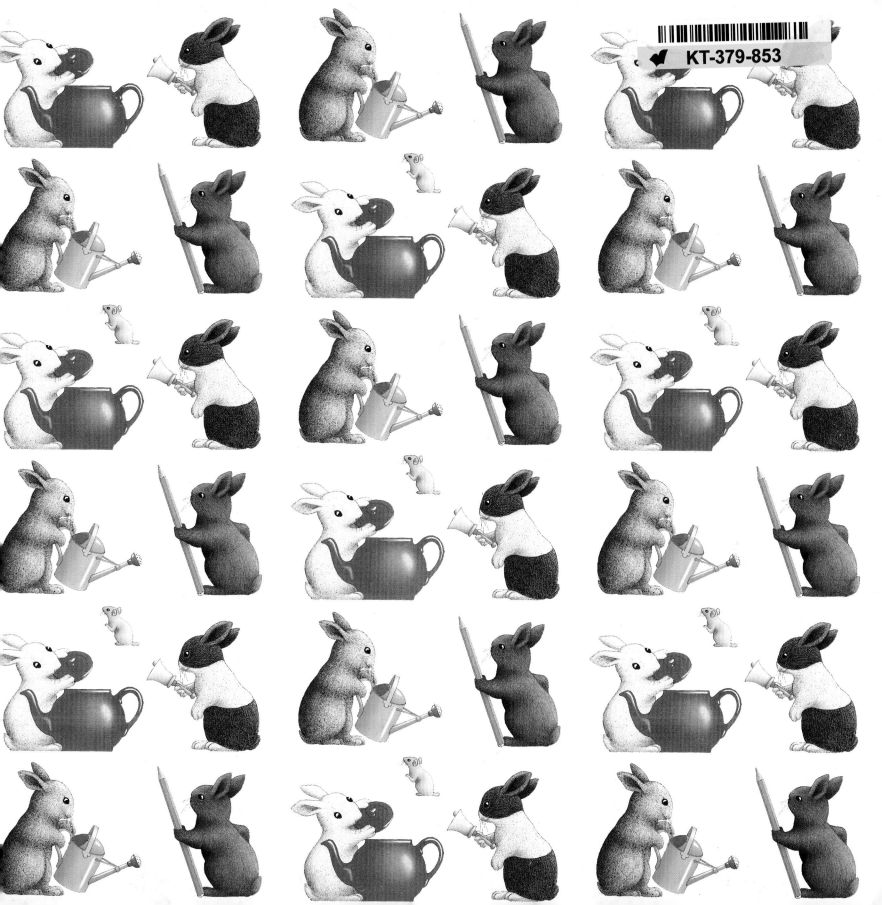

Note to parents

This book contains a wealth of beautiful illustrations showing familiar objects which young children will enjoy identifying.

You will also find numerous opportunities to introduce concepts such as colour, shape and number. You can help to reinforce your child's early learning skills by playing some of the games suggested on pages 36-37.

Talking about pictures is an excellent way to help your child develop verbal fluency and a rich vocabulary. By drawing attention to favourite words, you can introduce the idea of printed language. Encourage your child to look at the details in the pictures. This visual skill will be important later for learning to read.

Remember – always go at your child's pace and give constant praise. Your help and encouragement will enable your child to make the most of the learning experiences this book has to offer.

KINGFISHER
An imprint of Larousse plc
Elsley House, 24-30 Great Titchfield Street
London W1P 7AD

First published by Kingfisher 1996
2 4 6 8 10 9 7 5 3 1

Copyright © Alan Baker 1996

A CIP catalogue record for this book
is available from the British Library

ISBN 0 7534 0055 3

Additional text by Kate Hayden
Designed by Caroline Johnson
Printed in Singapore

Little Rabbits' Picture Word Book

Alan Baker

Kingfisher

Clothes

shoes

cap

socks

buttons

jacket

shirt

pants

jumper

dress

trousers

waistcoat

boots

7

In the kitchen

cup

plate

saucer

teapot

mug

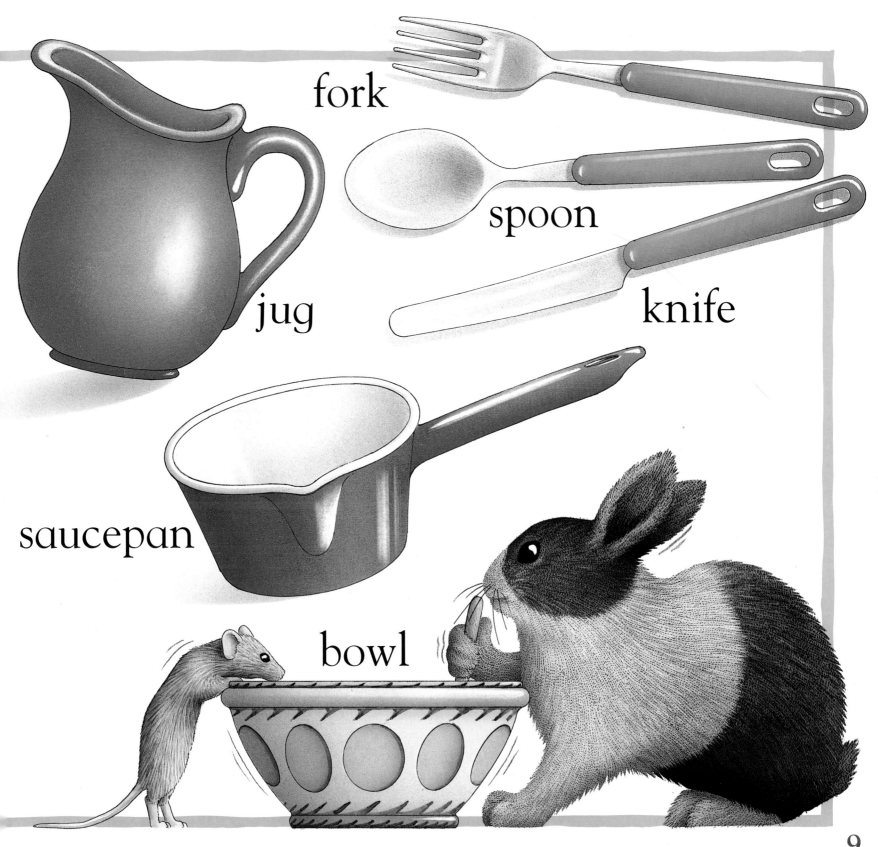

fork

spoon

jug

knife

saucepan

bowl

9

Toys

telephone

doll

toddle
truck

blocks

rattle

puzzle

beads

cards

pull-along train

11

Animals

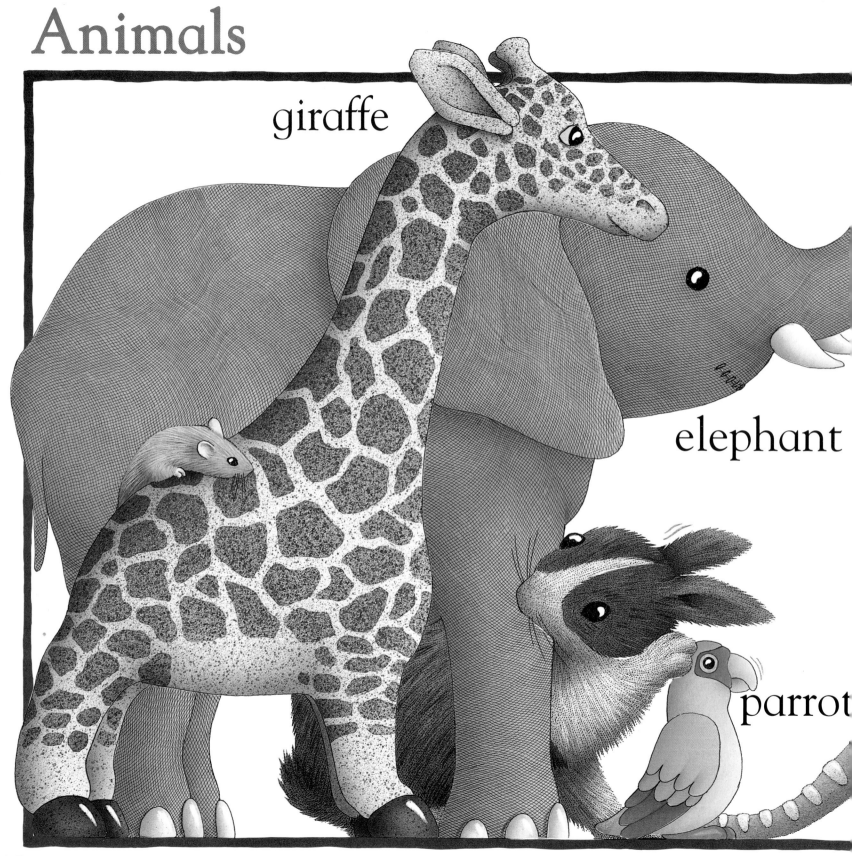

giraffe

elephant

parrot

tiger

monkey

crocodile

kangaroo

lion

panda

zebra

snake

13

Around the house

books

cushion

keys

dustpan

brush

broom

flower

flower
pot

leaf

watering can

rake

17

Making a noise

whistle

recorder

drum

flute

tambourine

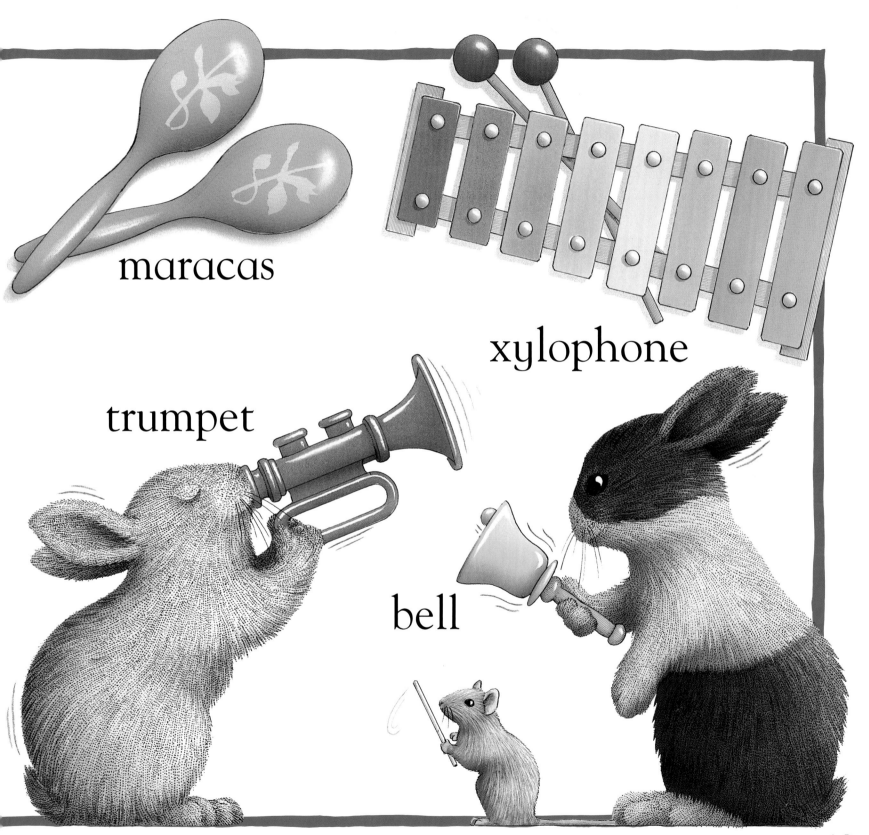

maracas

xylophone

trumpet

bell

19

Drawing and painting

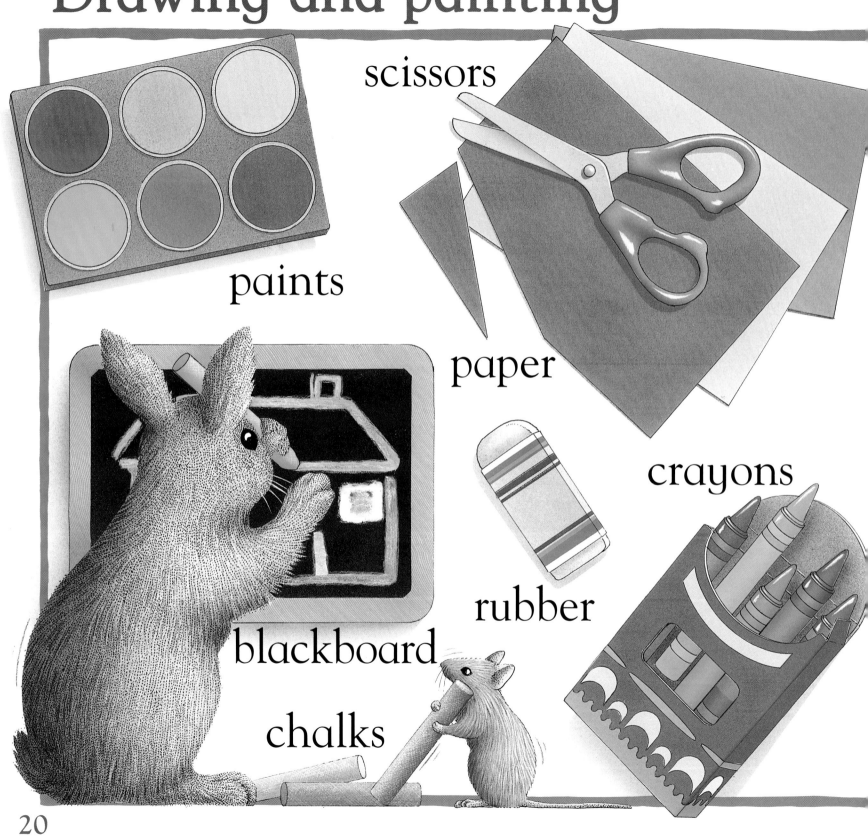

scissors

paints

paper

crayons

rubber

blackboard

chalks

20

ruler

felt-tip pens

paintbrushes

pencil

easel

21

Colours

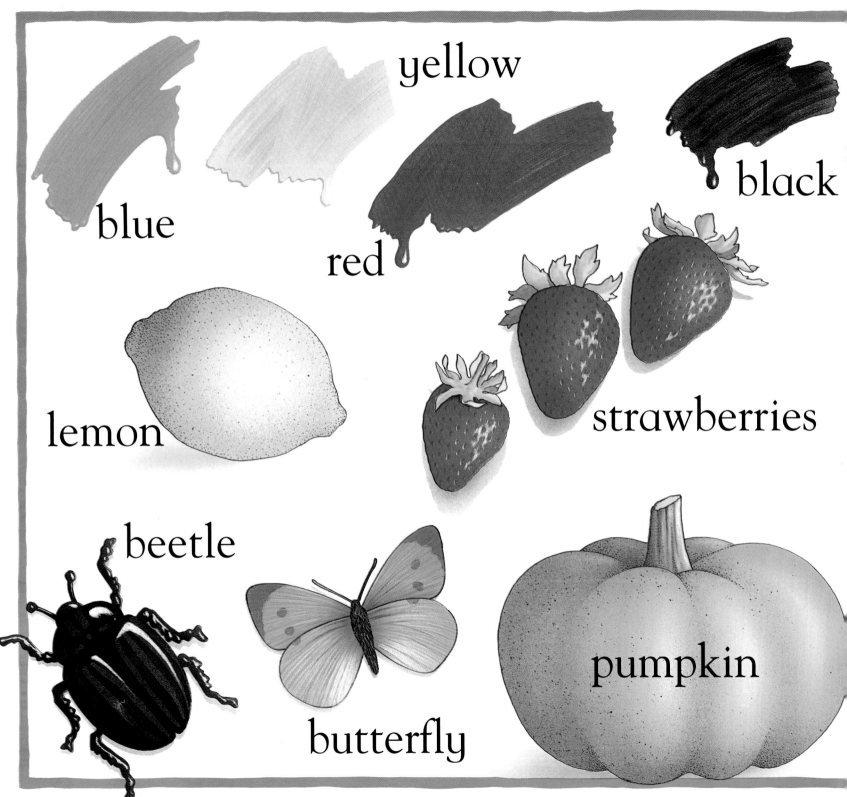

yellow

blue

black

red

lemon

strawberries

beetle

butterfly

pumpkin

22

purple

brown

green

orange

rabbit

frog

grapes

23

Shapes

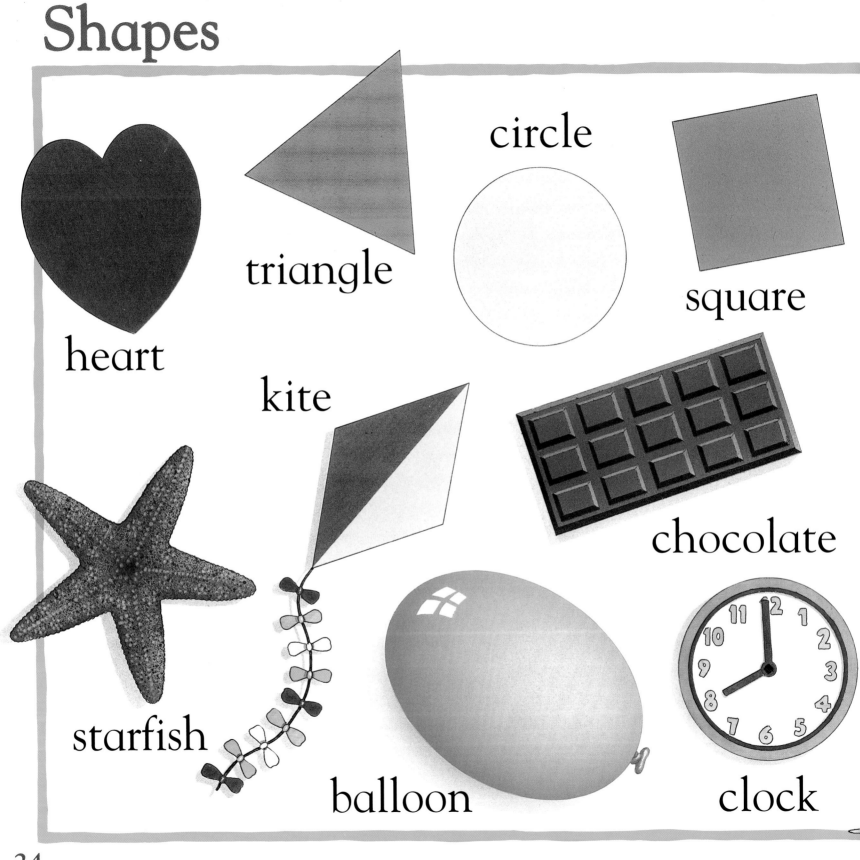

heart

triangle

circle

square

kite

chocolate

starfish

balloon

clock

24

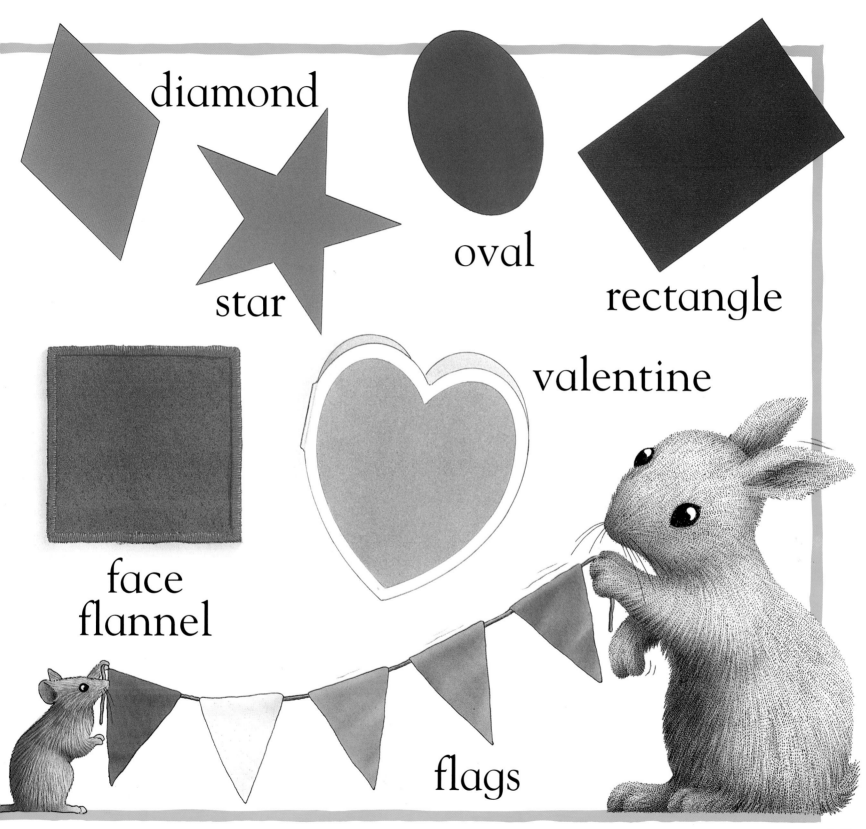

diamond

oval

rectangle

star

valentine

face
flannel

flags

25

At the park

umbrella

swing

bench

bicycle

tree

slide

seesaw

27

Things to eat

biscuits

sandwich

apple

banana

carrots

cheese

orange

noodles

sweetcorn

tomato

yoghurt

lettuce

ice-cream

On the farm

chicks

pig

horse

cow

goat

cockerel

dog

duck

hen

sheep

tractor

31

Bathtime

toothbrush

toothpaste

sponge

comb

shampoo

shower

towel

hairbrush

bubbles

soap

talcum
powder

mirror

bath

Bedtime

quilt

slippers

dressing gown

blanket

pyjamas

mobile

bed

duvet

pillow

teddy

35

Games to play

Playing these games with your child makes learning to recognize colours and shapes more fun and will help develop observation, verbal, sorting and matching skills.

Where's mouse?
Ask your child to look for the little brown mouse that appears on every double page. Help him or her to describe what the mouse is doing in each scene.

Who says moo? (pages 30-31)
Very young children love identifying and imitating animal noises. See if your child can find the animal to match the noises you make. Alternatively, point to an animal and ask your child to make the right noise.

Colour match (pages 22-23)
Ask your child to say what is blue on these pages. Continue through the other six colours, matching each brush stroke to the fruit or animal of the same colour.

Shape match (pages 24-25)
Help your child to find an object to match each of the two-dimensional shapes shown at the top of these pages. Introduce the names of some of the shapes, if you like.

What is round?
Help your child to look for round shapes or circles on some pages. Examples are: buttons (page 6), plate (page 8), beads, train wheels (pages 10-11), tambourine (page 18), paint box colours (page 20), circle and clock (page 24), wheels (page 26), bubbles (page 33).

Big and little (pages 12-13)
Ask your child which is the biggest animal and which is the smallest on this double page. Extend the discussion to other characteristics, for example: Who can fly? Who has stripes? Who can jump?

Match up the words
and pictures.

ant
ball
cushion
drum
fork
hairbrush
jug
kite
leaf
orange
paints
shoes
telephone
worm
yoghurt

37